CATS
WITH GUNS

CATS
WITH GUNS

Jonathan Parkyn

APPLE

First published in the UK by
Apple Press
7 Greenland Street
London NW1 0ND
United Kingdom
www.apple-press.com

ISBN: 978 1 84543 367 3

Editorial and design by
Amber Books Ltd. in London, UK
www.amberbooks.co.uk

Project Editor: James Bennett
Text: Jonathan Parkyn
Photoshop: Rajdip Sanghera
Layout Design: Rick Fawcett
Military Consultants: Chris McNab, Lewis Jones

Front cover photo credits: © Maine Coon (Dreamstime/Elena Butinova)
with AKS-74U (Photos.com) Target: Dreamstime/Antonevich Anastasia

Printed and bound in China

10 9 8 7 6 5 4 3 2 1

CONTENTS

RIDDLE OF THE SPHYNX

SPHYNX

A modern ancestor of the giant Sphinx that watched over the Great Pyramids of Giza, in Egypt, the hairless Sphynx has a cat's head rather than a human one and, instead of being made of stone, it's made of cat.

Breed	Sphynx
Country	Brunei
Origin	Natural breed
Body type	Medium, long
Coat type	Hairless
Pattern	None, it's hairless!
Personality	Inquisitive, friendly

BERETTA MODEL 92

A natural evolution from earlier Berettas, the 92 is a short-recoil locked-breech semi-automatic with an aluminium frame. If you have a pyramid or anything else you need to guard, the 92 is the gun for you.

Origin	United States
Calibre	9mm Parabellum
Operation	Short recoil
Weight	1kg
Overall length	197mm
Barrel length	109mm
Muzzle velocity	385m/sec

TOUGH FLUFF

BALINESE

If you're feeling uncharitable, you might dismiss the Balinese as little more than a fluffier Siamese – just don't let him hear you say that when he's pointing a semi-automatic in your direction.

Breed	Balinese
Country	Unknown
Origin	Natural breed
Body type	Long
Coat type	Medium to long
Pattern	Colourpoint
Personality	Affectionate

MAUSER C96

Introduced towards the end of the nineteenth century, the Mauser C96 was, as the name suggests, a German-made pistol originally designed for shooting mice, hence its enduring popularity in the feline world.

Origin	Germany
Calibre	7.63 or 9mm
Operation	Short recoil
Weight	1.2kg
Overall length	308mm
Barrel length	140mm
Muzzle velocity	433m/sec

KITTY KITTY BANG BANG

SIBERIAN

Don't be fooled by the cuddly fur-ball exterior and hypoallergenic qualities; years of hard labour in Soviet gulags have made the Siberian one tough customer – especially when it's packing some serious World War II hardware.

Breed	Siberian
Country	Russia
Origin	Natural breed
Body type	Large
Coat type	Semi-long
Pattern	Various
Personality	Loyal

MP40

Surely one of the most instantly recognizable submachine guns of all time, the open-bolt MP40 is the automatic weapon of choice for Nazi paratroopers and felines with fascistic leanings everywhere.

Origin	Germany
Calibre	9mm Parabellum
Operation	Blowback
Weight	4.0kg
Overall length	832mm
Barrel length	248mm
Muzzle velocity	380m/sec

Dressed To Kill

RAGAMUFFIN

The word 'ragamuffin' might make you think of scruffily dressed urchins or perhaps a style of music that fuses reggae with dance beats. In fact, the type of ragamuffin we're talking about here is neither. It's a cat.

Breed	Ragamuffin
Country	United States
Origin	Crossbreed
Body type	Large
Coat type	Semi-long to long
Pattern	Various
Personality	Affectionate

1863 REMINGTON

No – not the gun used by Remington Steele before he transformed into James Bond; this vintage .36- or .44-calibre revolver was actually the preferred firearm of Union troops during the American Civil War.

Origin	United States
Calibre	.36 or .44
Operation	Single action
Weight	1.3kg
Overall length	348mm
Barrel length	203mm
Muzzle velocity	213m/sec

13

Shoot First, Meow Later

ABYSSINIAN

Abyssinians – or 'Abys' as they are often called for short – have beautiful almond-shaped eyes and broad, pointed ears. Their slender, lithe physique and stealthy, athletic abilities make them excellent cat burglars.

Breed	Abyssinian
Country	Possibly Egypt
Origin	Natural breed
Body type	Muscular
Coat type	Short to medium
Pattern	Ticked
Personality	Extrovert

VICKERS HMG

A sturdy British-made .303-inch machine gun, the Vickers is a classic infantry weapon that saw service in two world wars and numerous, smaller conflicts that followed. (Note: requires at least two cats to operate.)

Origin	United Kingdom
Calibre	.303
Operation	Short recoil
Weight	9.4kg
Overall length	1155mm
Barrel length	723mm
Muzzle velocity	745m/sec

15

JURASSIC CLASSIC

CORNISH REX

Almost certainly a direct descendant of the fearsome *Tyrannosaurus rex*, this unusual breed has no outer fur—just a soft, wavy undercoat, which makes it better suited to people who suffer from cat (or dinosaur) allergies.

Breed	Cornish Rex
Country	United Kingdom
Origin	Natural mutation
Body type	Medium
Coat type	Short
Pattern	Various
Personality	Inquisitive

MAUSER M98

With its beech wood stock and bolt action, this rifle might look like a dinosaur itself, but the Mauser M98 is in reality a contemporary weapon that's often used by safari-hunting cats on the lookout for big game.

Origin	Germany
Calibre	.375 H&H and others
Operation	Bolt action
Weight	3.5kg
Overall length	1160mm
Barrel length	600mm
Muzzle velocity	Varies with calibre

1 2 3 4 5 6

17

AN OFFER YOU CAN'T REFUSE

DON SPHYNX

He might be almost completely hairless, but the 'Don' Sphynx is the Godfather of the cat family and must be shown due respect – unless you want to wind up sleeping with the goldfishes.

Breed	Don Sphynx
Country	Russia
Origin	Crossbreed
Body type	Medium
Coat type	Hairless
Pattern	None, it's hairless!
Personality	Friendly

M1928 THOMPSON

The unmistakable M1928 Thompson submachine gun – or 'tommy gun' – is the original mobster's weapon, as wielded by famous Dons including Don Corleone, Don Johnson (probably) and Don Rumsfeld (possibly).

Origin	United States
Calibre	.45
Operation	Delayed blowback
Weight	4.9kg
Overall length	857mm
Barrel length	266mm
Muzzle velocity	280m/sec

A Taste of the Orient

ORIENTAL SHORTHAIR

An elegant, streamlined creature, the Oriental Shorthair is not unlike what a classic '76 Alfa Romeo Spider may have looked like if it were a cat and not a car. Its rather large ears make ear-defenders a must on the shooting range.

Breed	Oriental Shorthair
Country	United Kingdom
Origin	Crossbreed
Body type	Long
Coat type	Short
Pattern	Various
Personality	Sociable

COLT DRAGOON

This .44-calibre single-action revolver was designed by Samuel Colt in 1848, and it was originally used by mounted US infantry, known as 'dragoons' (although they actually rode on horses, not on dragons).

Origin	United States
Calibre	.44
Operation	Single-action
Weight	1.9kg
Overall length	375mm
Barrel length	191mm
Muzzle velocity	335m/sec

Star Paws

KURILIAN BOBTAIL

Kurilians have dense, fine fur and a short 'bob' tail. They are said to originate from Russia's far eastern Kuril Islands, although if you're at the wrong end of a Walther PPK it's best not to question a cat's origins.

Breed	Kurilian Bobtail
Country	Russia
Origin	Natural breed
Body type	Semi-cobby
Coat type	Short or long
Pattern	Various
Personality	Intelligent

WALTHER PPK

Another weapon originating from Nazi Germany, this 1935 semi-automatic was also famous as James Bond's trademark pistol in Ian Fleming's original novels. The 'PPK' in the name stands for 'Please Protect Kurilians'.

Origin	Germany
Calibre	9mm Short
Operation	Blowback
Weight	0.6kg
Overall length	155mm
Barrel length	86mm
Muzzle velocity	280m/sec

TRUE BRIT

BRITISH LONGHAIR

Not to be confused with the British Shorthair, which is completely different (it has shorter hair, for a start), British Longhairs can be slightly snobbish and often come with bad teeth and stiff upper whiskers.

Breed	British Longhair
Country	United Kingdom
Origin	Natural breed
Body type	Stocky
Coat type	Long
Pattern	Various
Personality	Adaptable

BROWNING M1919

With a rate of fire between 400 and 600 rounds per minute, the belt-fed air-cooled M1919 was an American classic that was mounted on aircraft, tanks, armoured cars and kitty litter trays right up until the 1970s.

Origin	United States
Calibre	.30
Operation	Short recoil
Weight	14.1kg
Overall length	1041mm
Barrel length	610mm
Muzzle velocity	853m/sec

TOUGH LITTLE MANX

MANX

Hmmm. This chap's definitely missing something. And, no, we haven't just airbrushed it out in Photoshop. Manx cats can be born with 'stubby', 'stumpy' or 'longy' tails, or without a tail at all ('rumpy' or 'dimple rumpy').

Breed	Manx
Country	Isle of Man, UK
Origin	Natural breed
Body type	Medium
Coat type	Short or long
Pattern	Various (often tabby)
Personality	Hunter

LES BAER AR.223

Fed up with all the other cats teasing you because you have no tail? Who better to help you to show them exactly who's boss than Mr Les Baer and his Custom Ultimate AR.223 Super Varmint rifle?

Origin	United States
Calibre	.223
Operation	Gas
Weight	4.45kg
Overall length	n/a
Barrel length	1574mm
Muzzle velocity	n/a

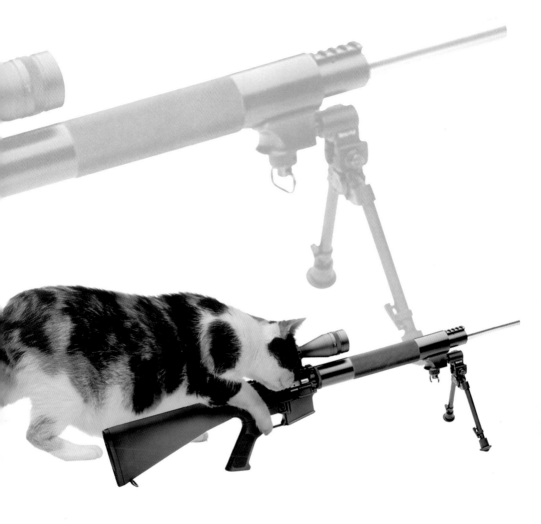

27

Hairless Hero

PETERBALD

The Peterbald cat is, as you may have expertly surmised from the name, a bald cat that is usually called Peter. A sweet-natured, intelligent animal, Peter is said to get on well with children, bald or otherwise.

Breed	Peterbald
Country	Russia
Origin	Crossbreed
Body type	Medium, long
Coat type	Various, usually hairless
Pattern	Various
Personality	Graceful

BROWN BESS INDIA PATTERN

Thinking of starting your own empire? Need a .75-calibre flintlock weapon to arm your troops? Look no further than the 1797 India Pattern – ideal for committing atrocities in the name of king and country.

Origin	United Kingdom
Calibre	0.75
Operation	Flintlock
Weight	4.5kg
Overall length	1378mm
Barrel length	921mm
Muzzle velocity	450m/sec

29

VIVE LA RÉSISTANCE!

CHARTREUX

One of the oldest officially recognized breeds in existence, the beautiful blue Chartreux is a sociable, intelligent and unequivocally French cat (briefly renamed 'Freedom Cat' during the Iraq conflict).

Breed	Chartreux
Country	France
Origin	Natural breed
Body type	Large
Coat type	Short
Pattern	Solid colour (blue)
Personality	Quiet

LUGER P08

When Georg Luger invented his iconic semi-automatic back in 1900, little did he know that it would end up being the official pistol of both the German Third Reich and French Resistance kitties, such as Monsieur Chartreux.

Origin	Germany
Calibre	9mm Parabellum
Operation	Short recoil
Weight	0.9kg
Overall length	222mm
Barrel length	103mm
Muzzle velocity	320m/sec

THE HOST WITH THE GHOST

SNOWSHOE

Thankfully for this particular feline, originally bred to be worn on the foot in cold weather, there are now special laws against using the Snowshoe as an actual snowshoe. Interestingly, baby Snowshoes are called 'kittens'.

Breed	Snowshoe
Country	United States
Origin	Crossbreed
Body type	Medium
Coat type	Short
Pattern	Colourpoint
Personality	Mellow

SPECTRE M4

Popular with armed forces, law enforcement agencies and civilians alike since the early 1980s, the Italian-built Spectre is so called because, at close range, you simply don't stand a ghost of a chance.

Origin	Italy
Calibre	9mm Parabellum
Operation	Blowback
Weight	2.9kg
Overall length	580mm
Barrel length	130mm
Muzzle velocity	400m/sec

Back to the Future

EUROPEAN SHORTHAIR

The European Shorthair is a muscular, well-proportioned cat from – yes, you guessed it – Europe with – that's right, you guessed it again – short hair. The current rate of exchange is 1 Euro Shorthair to 1.46 American Shorthairs.

Breed	European Shorthair
Country	Sweden
Origin	Natural breed
Body type	Medium to large
Coat type	Short
Pattern	Various
Personality	Hunter

XM29 OICW

The XM29 is a glimpse into the future – a prototype developed for the US Army's discontinued Objective Individual Combat Weapons (OICW) programme. It features night vision, a grenade launcher and an iPod dock.

Origin	United States
Calibre	5.56 x 45mm/20mm
Operation	Gas
Weight	5.5kg
Overall length	890mm
Barrel length	250mm
Muzzle velocity	n/a

Separated at Birth

SIAMESE

Contrary to popular misconception, these elegant cats from Southeast Asia do not always come in sets of twins. Ice blue almond eyes and seal (brown) or gray points give the Siamese its distinctive killer look.

Breed	Siamese
Country	Thailand
Origin	Natural breed
Body type	Medium, slim
Coat type	Short
Pattern	Colourpoint
Personality	Very vocal

SPAS-12

A semi-automatic or pump-action shotgun of Italian origin, the SPAS-12 is a versatile, reliable weapon with plenty of firepower, although its weight (4.2kg) makes it suitable only for bodybuilders and battle cats.

Origin	Italy
Calibre	12-gauge
Operation	Gas/pump-action
Weight	4.2kg
Overall length	1041mm
Barrel length	460mm
Muzzle velocity	n/a

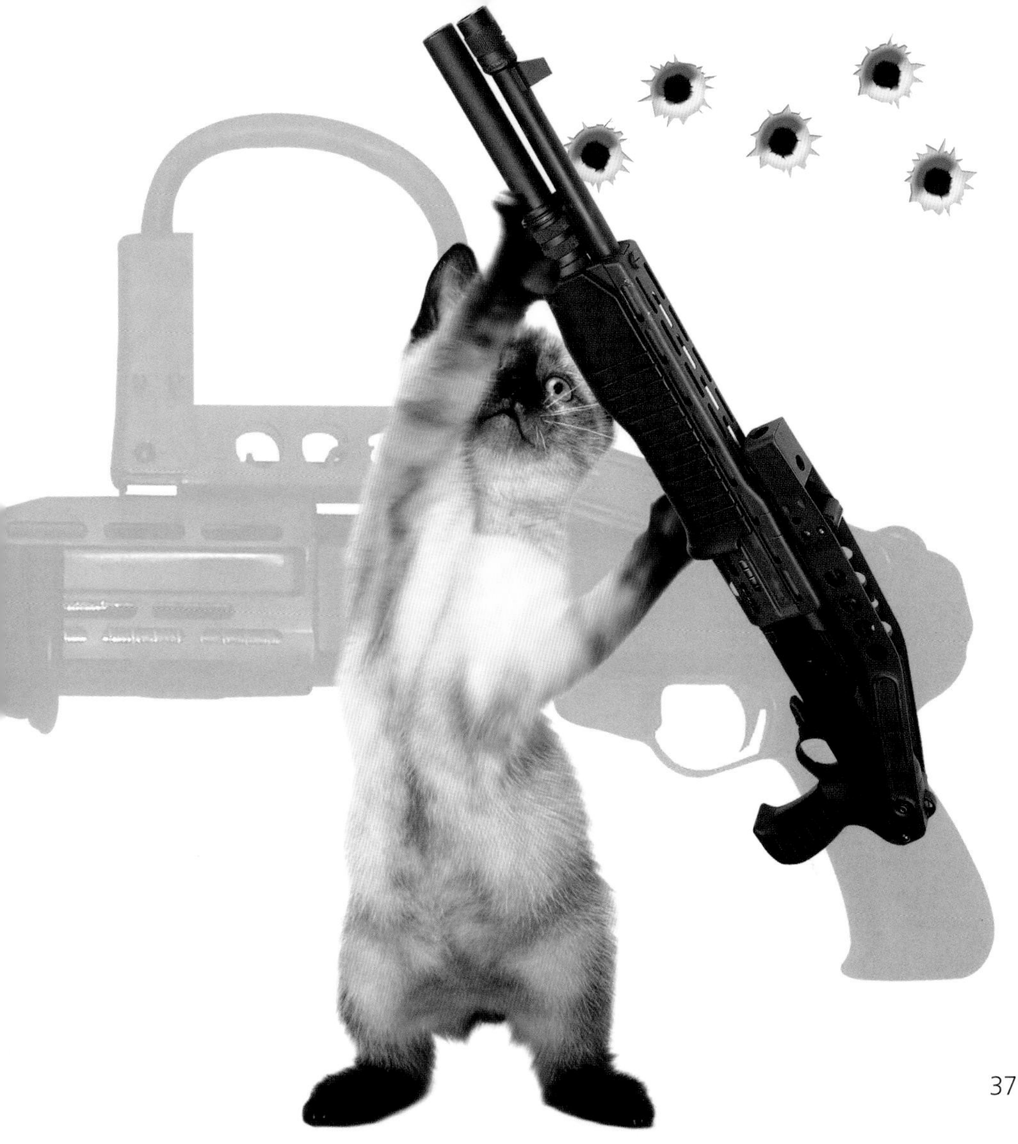

TOM AND JERRY

BURMESE

The Burmese is a friendly, talkative breed with a glossy coat, typically sable (brown) in colour. It's unusual for the highly sociable and rarely aggressive Burmese to discharge a firearm unless provoked.

Breed	Burmese
Country	Thailand
Origin	Natural breed
Body type	Medium
Coat type	Short
Pattern	Various, usually brown
Personality	Affectionate

WALTHER P38

A German 9mm semi-automatic with an eight-round detachable single-stack magazine feed system. Dating back to the start of World War II, the P38 remains a standard-issue pistol for Walther Kitties the world over.

Origin	Germany
Calibre	9mm Short
Operation	Short recoil
Weight	1kg
Overall length	219mm
Barrel length	124mm
Muzzle velocity	350m/sec

HANUKKAH MATATA

SERENGETI

Although it is named after the geographical region made famous by *The Lion King*, the Serengeti has little in common with the big cats you might find prowling there. It rarely sings Elton John songs, for example.

Breed	Serengeti
Country	United States
Origin	Crossbreed
Body type	Medium, long
Coat type	Short
Pattern	Spotted or solid black
Personality	Self-assured

IMI NEGEV

A light belt-fed machine gun, the IMI Negev is also named after a place – the dry, barren regions of the Negev in southern Israel – which makes it the ideal weapon for desert cats such as Mr Serengeti.

Origin	Israel
Calibre	5.56 x 45mm NATO
Operation	Gas
Weight	7.2kg
Overall length	1020mm
Barrel length	460mm
Muzzle velocity	950m/sec

GLAMOUR PUSS

EXOTIC SHORTHAIR

Have you ever wondered what would happen if you put an American Shorthair and an exotic Persian cat in a machine like the one Jeff Goldblum had at his disposal in *The Fly*, and pressed the 'oops' button?

Breed	Exotic Shorthair
Country	United States
Origin	Crossbreed
Body type	Cobby
Coat type	Short
Pattern	Various
Personality	Calm, playful

FALLSCHIRM-JÄGERGEWEHR 42

Lightweight and adaptable, the Fallschirmjägergewehr 42 can do the job of a machine gun, grenade launcher and sniper rifle all in one – just don't try saying its name when you're coughing up a fur ball.

Origin	Germany
Calibre	7.92 x 57mm Mauser
Operation	Gas
Weight	4.5kg
Overall length	940mm
Barrel length	502mm
Muzzle velocity	761m/sec

43

ON YOUR MARKS!

SELKIRK REX

While it may look as if someone has accidentally left it out in the rain, the Selkirk Rex is a naturally curly-haired and very athletic breed – the one seen here, for example, is firing a pistol to start a race.

Breed	Selkirk Rex
Country	United States
Origin	Crossbreed
Body type	Medium
Coat type	Short or long, curly
Pattern	Various
Personality	Patient, loving

SMITH & WESSON .38

Like the Selkirk Rex, the Smith & Wesson .38 is small yet powerful. Unlike the Selkirk Rex, the revolver is completely hairless, has a carbon steel frame and fires bullets instead of saying 'meow'.

Origin	United States
Calibre	.38 Special
Operation	Revolver
Weight	0.4kg
Overall length	165mm
Barrel length	51mm
Muzzle velocity	260m/sec

Bad Boys

DEVON REX

Playful, bold and highly active in temperament, the Devon Rex has a unique appearance – it has very short hair and large, sticky-out ears that effectively make it the feline version of Hollywood hero Will Smith.

Breed	Devon Rex
Country	United Kingdom
Origin	Natural breed
Body type	Medium
Coat type	Short
Pattern	Various
Personality	Mischievous

COLT M4 CARBINE

The highly compact American-made M4 Carbine assault rifle is used by military and law enforcement agencies around the world – as well as by the human version of Will Smith in the blockbuster film *I Am Legend*.

Origin	United States
Calibre	5.56 x 45mm NATO
Operation	Gas
Weight	2.7kg
Overall length	838mm
Barrel length	368mm
Muzzle velocity	880m/sec

47

GLOBAL CAT-ASTROPHE

BIRMAN

Unlike the Burmese (which, despite what its name suggests, comes from Thailand), the Birman does originate from Burma. In fact, it is also known as the 'Sacred Cat of Burma' because of its firm religious beliefs.

Breed	Birman
Country	Burma
Origin	Natural breed
Body type	Medium
Coat type	Semi-long
Pattern	Various (often colourpoint)
Personality	Playful

BROWNING 1910

Browning's compact semi-automatic pistol famously kick-started World War I. Its easily concealable nature has made it the covert weapon of choice among assassins, saboteurs, double agents and spy cats ever since.

Origin	Belgium
Calibre	7.7mm or 9mm
Operation	Blowback
Weight	0.6kg
Overall length	154mm
Barrel length	88.5mm
Muzzle velocity	299m/sec

49

POINT 'N' SHOOT

TURKISH ANGORA

Outgoing, intelligent and affectionate in nature, the distinctive pointy-eared Turkish Angora has the remarkable attribute of being one of the only cat breeds known to have been named after a type of woollen garment.

Breed	Turkish Angora
Country	Turkey
Origin	Natural breed
Body type	Medium, slim
Coat type	Semi-long
Pattern	Various (except colourpoint)
Personality	Outgoing

M14

Used extensively by US forces throughout the Vietnam War and beyond, the M14 rifle is almost uncontrollable in fully automatic mode, but its high power makes it ideal for jungle cats of all varieties.

Origin	United States
Calibre	7.62 x 51mm NATO
Operation	Gas
Weight	3.9kg
Overall length	1120mm
Barrel length	559mm
Muzzle velocity	853m/sec

WHERE THE WILD THINGS ARE

CALIFORNIA SPANGLED

Don't panic – it's not a leopard! It's a California Spangled, which, although spotted, is much smaller than a leopard and much less dangerous – unless, of course, it happens to be carrying a 12-gauge shotgun.

Breed	Californian Spangled
Country	United States
Origin	Crossbreed
Body type	Long
Coat type	Short
Pattern	Spotted (various colours)
Personality	Hunter

LANBER SPORTER

The popular Spanish-made Lanber Sporter is a simple, dependable and, above all, powerful firearm. If you really want to give the cat a chance to shoot some clay pigeons – or rubber chickens – accept no substitute.

Origin	Spain
Calibre	12-gauge
Operation	Break-open
Weight	3.5kg
Overall length	n/a
Barrel length	720mm
Muzzle velocity	n/a

WALK LIKE AN EGYPTIAN

EGYPTIAN MAU

MOSSBERG 500

Today's moggies are believed to have originated in Ancient Egypt, so if ever there was a prototype for the modern domestic kitty it would probably be the Mau, images of which can be clearly seen in early Egyptian graffiti.

Ancient Egyptians didn't have pump-action shotguns but, if they did, the 12-gauge Mossberg 500 would probably have been just the thing to help them encourage their slaves to build more pyramids.

Breed	Egyptian Mau
Country	Egypt
Origin	Natural breed
Body type	Medium
Coat type	Short
Pattern	Spotted
Personality	Loyal

Origin	United States
Calibre	12-gauge
Operation	Pump-action
Weight	3.5kg
Overall length	1238mm
Barrel length	720mm
Muzzle velocity	n/a

STONE COLD KILLER

NORWEGIAN FOREST

Long-haired, fluffy-coated, bushy-tailed and highly resistant to cold, harsh Scandinavian climates, the Norwegian Forest is one of the few cat breeds that the Beatles sort of wrote a song about.

Breed	Norwegian Forest
Country	Norway
Origin	Natural breed
Body type	Large
Coat type	Semi-long
Pattern	Various
Personality	Low-maintenance

AK-47

Also perfectly adapted for extreme weather conditions is the Soviet-designed Kalashnikov assault rifle – the AK-47. From the jungles of Vietnam to the mountains of Central Asia, nothing says 'insurrection' quite like it.

Origin	USSR/Russia
Calibre	7.62 x 39mm
Operation	Gas
Weight	5.1kg
Overall length	869mm
Barrel length	414mm
Muzzle velocity	710m/sec

57

ARE YOU TONKING TO ME?

TONKINESE

Blending the distinctive looks of the Siamese with the fun-loving nature of the Burmese, the Tonkinese is the 'best of both worlds'. Tonks can be very vocal and are, of course, fluent in Tonkinese.

Breed	Tonkinese
Country	United States
Origin	Crossbreed
Body type	Medium
Coat type	Short
Pattern	Various (usually colourpoint)
Personality	Strong-willed

COLT M1911A1

An early semi-automatic pistol, the 1911 enjoyed a lengthy military service. It's still popular today, though many 1911s in circulation these days are 'clones', made with DNA obtained from genuine Colt stem cells.

Origin	United States
Calibre	.45 ACP
Operation	Short recoil
Weight	1.4kg
Overall length	219mm
Barrel length	128mm
Muzzle velocity	252m/sec

59

HELLO, DOLLY

RAGDOLL

The confusing name might lead you to assume that cats of this type are stitched together from leftover bits of other cat – in fact, Ragdolls are so named because of their floppy, docile temperament.

Breed	Ragdoll
Country	United States
Origin	Crossbreed
Body type	Medium to large, long
Coat type	Semi-long
Pattern	Mitted or colourpoint
Personality	Placid

ARMSCOR M30R6

This pump-action shotgun from the Philippines comes with an affordable price tag and is suitable for a wide range of uses, including home or self-defence, law enforcement and zombie decapitation.

Origin	Philippines
Calibre	12-gauge
Operation	Pump-action
Weight	3.5kg
Overall length	1193mm
Barrel length	470mm
Muzzle velocity	n/a

61

Bit of a Long Shot

BURMILLA

Bred accidentally in 1981, the Burmilla is, as you might expect from the name, a cross between a Burmese and a gorilla (although it is possible that we may have that gorilla part the teensiest bit wrong).

Breed	Burmilla
Country	United Kingdom
Origin	Crossbreed
Body type	Medium
Coat type	Short, semi-long, long
Pattern	Various
Personality	Sociable

ENFIELD-SNIDER 1860

This antique British breech-loading rifle was unusually long – even for its time – allowing infantry to poke the enemy right in the eye from all the way across the battlefield, as well as shoot at them.

Origin	United Kingdom
Calibre	.577
Operation	Hinged breech
Weight	3.7kg
Overall length	1219mm
Barrel length	838mm
Muzzle velocity	355m/sec

HERE COME THE CURLS

AMERICAN CURL

Available in both long- and short-haired varieties, American Curls can be distinguished by their ears, which 'curl' back to give them a somewhat startled appearance – something that sometimes they really are.

Breed	American Curl
Country	United States
Origin	Natural mutation
Body type	Medium
Coat type	Short or long
Pattern	Various
Personality	Dog-like

LEWIS GUN

This vintage light machine gun also has its own distinctive look – there are no curled ears this time, though (guns don't have ears). It's the top-mounted pan magazine that makes the Lewis instantly recognizable.

Origin	Belgium/USA/UK
Calibre	.303
Operation	Gas
Weight	11.8kg
Overall length	1250mm
Barrel length	661mm
Muzzle velocity	744m/sec

65

Ratta-Tat-Cat

OCICAT

A larger-than-average, athletic breed, the spotted Ocicat looks a lot like an ocelot. With its jungle cat reflexes and natural camouflage, the Ocicat is the ideal candidate for manning (or 'catting') machine-gun emplacements.

Breed	Ocicat
Country	United States
Origin	Crossbreed
Body type	Medium to large, long
Coat type	Short
Pattern	Spotted
Personality	Devoted

CHAUCHAT

The name of this French machine gun literally translates as 'hot cat'. Unfortunately, it was also possibly the least reliable weapon of World War I, usually becoming too 'hot' itself after firing just a few rounds.

Origin	France
Calibre	8 x 50mmR Lebel
Operation	Long recoil
Weight	9.07kg
Overall length	1143mm
Barrel length	496mm
Muzzle velocity	700m/sec

PUSSY GALORE

MAINE COON

This long-haired cat, weighing in at up to 10kg, is one of the oldest breeds in North America. The Maine Coon's ability to disguise itself as a Russian fur hat made it ideal for undercover ops during the Cold War.

Breed	Maine Coon
Country	United States
Origin	Natural breed
Body type	Classic
Coat type	Long
Pattern	Various (except colourpoint)
Personality	Individualist

AKS-74U

Take the original Kalashnikov AKS-74, shorten the carbine, move the gas chamber, lower the front sight base and what have you got? A compact assault rifle that's very cool for cats, that's what!

Origin	USSR/Russia
Calibre	5.45 x 39mm
Operation	Gas
Weight	2.5kg
Overall length	943mm
Barrel length	210mm
Muzzle velocity	900m/sec

69

Rinky Dink Panther

BOMBAY

With its sleek black coat, the muscular and agile Bombay may well look like a miniature panther, but in temperament it's actually more like a dog; it plays fetch, sits on your lap and answers to the name 'Fido'.

Breed	Bombay
Country	United States
Origin	Crossbreed
Body type	Medium
Coat type	Short
Pattern	Solid colour (black)
Personality	Dog-like

GARAND M1

If World War II had been fought by pets (instead of people), then this .30-calibre semi-automatic classic is precisely what US Army cats would have used to defeat all those evil Nazi dogs.

Origin	United States
Calibre	.30-06
Operation	Gas
Weight	4.313kg
Overall length	1107mm
Barrel length	609mm
Muzzle velocity	855m/sec

71

PUSSY POSSE

NON-PEDIGREE

COLT FRONTIER PEACEMAKER

The American 'Wild West' was a place where men were real men, women were real women, and cats were real cats. This young ginger tom, for example, is 100 per cent cat, with no artificial flavourings or additives.

No cow cat worth his chaps would be seen dead with anything less than this .45 at his furry hip. Designed as an army service revolver in 1873, the Peacemaker actually didn't make much peace at all.

Breed	n/a
Country	n/a
Origin	Natural cross
Body type	Various
Coat type	Short, long, semi-long
Pattern	Various
Personality	Various

Origin	United States
Calibre	.45
Operation	Single-action revolver
Weight	1kg
Overall length	279mm
Barrel length	140mm
Muzzle velocity	198m/sec

Say Hello to My Little Friend

PERSIAN

Think of the cutest thing you could possibly imagine and the chances are it won't be anywhere near as cute as a Persian cat. Unless, of course, the thing that you thought of originally actually was a Persian cat.

Breed	Persian
Country	Iran
Origin	Natural breed
Body type	Medium to large
Coat type	Long
Pattern	Various
Personality	Gentle

M16A1

A US military assault rifle in the 1960s and 1970s, the M16A1 also happens to be the weapon with which, at the end of the film *Scarface*, Al Pacino tries ever so politely to persuade his visitors to leave his home.

Origin	United States
Calibre	5.56 x 45mm NATO
Operation	Gas
Weight	3.99kg
Overall length	1006mm
Barrel length	508mm
Muzzle velocity	853m/sec

SHOT TO THE HEART

SINGAPURA

Undemanding and independent, the Singapura is the ultimate low-maintenance household pet. He likes to keep himself clean, is easy to litter-train and has even been known to file his own taxes.

Breed	Singapura
Country	Singapore
Origin	Natural breed
Body type	Small
Coat type	Short
Pattern	Ivory with sable ticking
Personality	Extrovert

COLT MT6601 HBAR

Everybody has their own take on the ArmaLite AR-15; the Colt MT6601 is just one of dozens of variants. The 'HBAR' part refers to the free Hershey Bar – or should that be a KitKat? – that comes with every rifle sold.

Origin	United States
Calibre	5.56 x 45mm NATO
Operation	Gas
Weight	3.63kg
Overall length	991mm
Barrel length	508mm
Muzzle velocity	975m/sec

(Less) Lethal Weapon

JAPANESE BOBTAIL

FN 303

Like a mythical beast, the Japanese Bobtail has the body of an average cat and the tail of a much smaller feline. Some legends say it was originally called 'Robert Tail' before both name and tail were shortened.

Riot guns such as the FN 303 are often referred to as 'less-lethal' weapons because they are technically 'less' lethal than other, properly lethal weapons – ideal if you're looking to make someone slightly less dead.

Breed	Japanese Bobtail
Country	Japan
Origin	Natural breed
Body type	Long, muscular
Coat type	Short
Pattern	Various
Personality	Chatty

Origin	Belgium
Calibre	12-gauge
Operation	Compressed air
Weight	2.3kg
Overall length	740mm
Barrel length	n/a
Muzzle velocity	Various

Small But
Purr-fectly Formed

MUNCHKIN

Contrary to popular belief, Munchkins don't come from the Land of Oz, but from Rayville, Louisiana. They have a feisty character, a plush, silky coat and unusually short legs – like a kind of 'Dachshund cat'.

Breed	Munchkin
Country	United States
Origin	Mutation
Body type	Small to medium
Coat type	Short or long
Pattern	Various
Personality	Playful

DERRINGER

If short and stubby is your thing, the Remington Derringer 1852 is the perfect sidearm to meet your needs. It's small but powerful and easily concealable, slipping comfortably under a loose fold of fur.

Origin	United States
Calibre	.41
Operation	Breech-loading
Weight	340g
Overall length	121mm
Barrel length	76mm
Muzzle velocity	137m/sec

Turkish Delight

TURKISH VAN

The Turkish Van is not very van-like at all. In fact, if you were going to name this furry feline specimen after a vehicle, then Turkish 'Boat' might have been more accurate, as it's one of the few cats that can swim.

Breed	Turkish Van
Country	Turkey
Origin	Natural breed
Body type	Long, sturdy
Coat type	Semi-long
Pattern	White with patches
Personality	Mischievous

RIFLE NO. 5 MK 1

Here's another misleading name; 'Rifle No. 5 Mk 1' makes this valiant vintage Lee-Enfield sound as exciting as a box of socks. Thankfully it's also known unofficially as the much less dull-sounding 'Jungle Carbine'.

Origin	United Kingdom
Calibre	.303
Operation	Bolt-action
Weight	3.25kg
Overall length	1003mm
Barrel length	476mm
Muzzle velocity	730m/sec

Hear My Roar!

NON-PEDIGREE

Most cats are sweet-natured, loveable balls of fur who love nothing more than a nice warm lap. Take away kitty's catnip, however, and you could wind up staring down the warm barrel of an MG42 instead.

Breed	n/a
Country	n/a
Origin	Natural cross
Body type	Various
Coat type	Short, long, semi-long
Pattern	Various
Personality	Various

MG42

Its name stands for 'Maschinengewehr 42' – literally, the '1942 machine gun'. There were other machine guns in 1942 but, at least as far as the Nazis were concerned, this was the only one that mattered.

Origin	Germany
Calibre	7.92 x 57mm Mauser
Operation	Short recoil
Weight	11.5kg
Overall length	1219mm
Barrel length	533mm
Muzzle velocity	755m/sec

A LOAD OF OLD BOLSHOI

RUSSIAN BLUE

The lithe and elegant Russian Blue has a long, lean body and a sleek, shimmering coat. Agile, sprightly felines, Blues are often said to make excellent Russian ballet and acrobat cats ('acrocats').

Breed	Russian Blue
Country	Russia
Origin	Natural breed
Body type	Medium, long
Coat type	Short
Pattern	Solid colour (blue)
Personality	Aristocratic

BERETTA 84F

Also known as the 'Cheetah', this Italian semi-automatic has an alloy frame, a double-stacked magazine that holds 13 rounds, and an ambidextrous safety, making it suitable for southpaw paws.

Origin	Italy
Calibre	9mm
Operation	Blowback
Weight	660g
Overall length	172mm
Barrel length	97mm
Muzzle velocity	280m/sec

Double Trouble

BRITISH SHORTHAIR

With slightly shorter hair than the British Longhair, the British Shorthair has many coat variants, including the 'blue', which isn't really blue (it's grey), and the 'tortoiseshell', which doesn't really have a tortoise shell.

Breed	British Shorthair
Country	United Kingdom
Origin	Natural breed
Body type	Large
Coat type	Short
Pattern	Various
Personality	Easygoing

M1917 REVOLVER

At one time manufactured by both Colt and Smith & Wesson, this definitive American six-shooter was issued to troops during World War I, and later became a firm favourite with civilians for deterring cat burglars.

Origin	United States
Calibre	.45 ACP
Operation	Double-action revolver
Weight	1.02kg
Overall length	274mm
Barrel length	140mm
Muzzle velocity	253m/sec

89

DUDE, WHERE'S MY GUN?

NON-PEDIGREE

Proving that you don't need a pedigree to be a top cat, here's one cool, dual-wielding kitty who could give Hollywood action stars such as Keanu Reeves a run for their money, particularly in the acting stakes.

Breed	n/a
Country	n/a
Origin	Natural cross
Body type	Various
Coat type	Short, long, semi-long
Pattern	Various
Personality	Various

UZI

If there's one weapon that has been in more movies than Morgan Freeman, it would have to be Israel's most famous submachine gun, the Uzi – star of *The Matrix*, *The Terminator* and virtually everything else.

Origin	Israel
Calibre	9mm Parabellum
Operation	Blowback
Weight	3.7kg
Overall length	650mm
Barrel length	260mm
Muzzle velocity	400m/sec

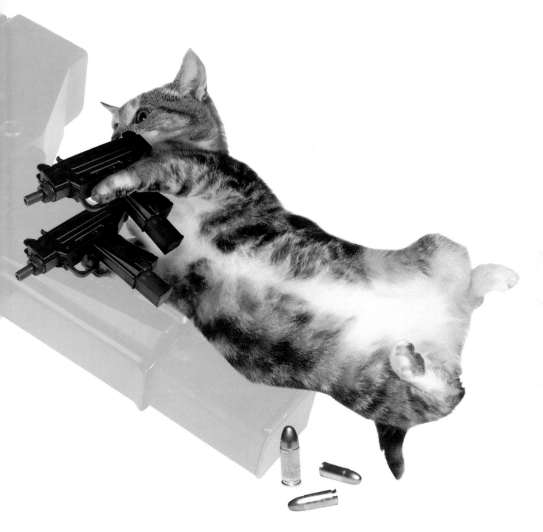

Salvation Orig-Army

SCOTTISH FOLD

A good-natured, intelligent and softly spoken breed, the Scottish Fold is so called because of its ability to fold paper into various shapes – swans, unicorns and sometimes even other breeds of cat.

Breed	Scottish Fold
Country	Scotland
Origin	Natural breed
Body type	Medium
Coat type	Short or long
Pattern	Various
Personality	Inquisitive

FN FAL

Belgium is known mainly for its waffles, its beer-making monks, its luxury chocolates and, of course, the Brussels sprout, but it is also home to a number of famous firearms, including this popular Cold War classic rifle.

Origin	Belgium
Calibre	7.62 x 51mm NATO
Operation	Gas
Weight	5kg
Overall length	1143mm
Barrel length	554mm
Muzzle velocity	838m/sec

Feline power grows out of
the barrel of a gun.
Meow Zedong

Whoever said that the pen is
mightier than the sword obviously
never encountered a kitten with an
automatic weapon.
General Douglas "Furball" MacArthur

And I swear that I don't have a
gun ... no, I don't have a gun.
Cat Cobain, "Come As You Are" by Purrvana

There it is, the AK-47. When you absolutely, positively, have to kill every single mouse in the room; accept no substitute.

Ordell Moggie, *Jackie Brown*

Guns will make us powerful; butter will only make us fat cats.

Hermann "Pussy" Göring

INDEX

PICTURE CREDITS